Animal Stories

Retold by
Sharon Hurst

Kapadokya ELT.
Retold by Sharon HURST
Typesetting & Design Metin AYDOĞAN
Pictures drawn by RÜZGÂR
Cover by Ali İMREN
Operating pressure HTC Offset Printing in Ankara
ISBN: 978-975-9944-124-50-8

Anafartalar Mah. Kazım Karabekir Caddesi Öğün İş Hanı No: 40/60
06050 İskitler-ALTINDAĞ / ANKARA Tel. & Fax: (+90312) 312 72 57
Web: www.kapadokyakitap.com • E-mail: info@kapadokyakitap.com

Kapadokya Readers

Easy Starters
* The Easter Egg Hunt, Sharon Hurst
* The Last Biscuit, Sharon Hurst
* The Christmas Turkey Mystery, Sharon Hurst
* The Football Match, Sharon Hurst
* Carol and Tom's Wedding, Sharon Hurst
* Hannah's New Bedroom, Sharon Hurst
* Jack's Driving Test Adventure, Sharon Hurst
* Jack's Wisdom Tooth, Sharon Hurst
* Mothers' Day, Sharon Hurst
* A Trip to London, Sharon Hurst
* Bonfire Night, Sharon Hurst
* Hasan's Visit, Sharon Hurst

Stage 1
* The Phoenix Bird and Other Tales, R. A. Green
* Gulliver's Travels, Jonathan Swift
* Persuasion, Jane Austen
* Peter Pan, James Matthew Barrie
* The Mermaid and Other Tales, Hans C. Andersen
* Animal Stories, Sharon Hurst
* Vegetable Stories, Sharon Hurst
* Stories About Food, Sharon Hurst
* Sam's New School, Sharon Hurst
* The Jones Family, Sharon Hurst

Stage 2
* Alice in Wonderland, Lewis Carroll
* Anne of the Green Gables, L. M. Montgomery

Stage 2 (suite)
* Stories From Edgar Allan Poe, Edgar Allan Poe
* Moby Dick, Herman Melville
* The Children of New Forest, Captain F. Marryat
* The School Holidays, Sharon Hurst

Stage 3
* Tom Sawyer, Mark Twain
* Huckle Berry Finn, Mark Twain
* Uncle Tom's Cabin, Harriet Beecher Stowe
* The Call of The Wild, Jack London
* The Picture of Dorian Gray, Oscar Wilde

Stage 4
* Short Stories,
* David Copperfield, Charles Dickens
* Oliver Twist, Charles Dickens
* Treasure Island, Robert L. Stevenson
* Jane Eyre, Charlotte Brontë

Stage 5
* Little Women, Louisa May Alcott
* Pride and Prejudice, Jane Austen
* Wuthering Heights, Emily Brontë
* Silas Marner, George Eliot
* The Thirty Nine Steps, John Buchan

Stage 6
* A Tale of Two Cities, Charles Dickens
* A Song of Six Pence, Archibald Joseph Cronin
* The Mystery of the Woman in the Mirror, Teri Martini
* The Pearl, John Steinbeck
* Great Expectations, Charles Dickens

Level: 1

The Three Billy Goats Gruff

Part 1

Once upon a time there were three billy goats. Their name was Gruff. There was Big billy goat Gruff, Middle billy goat Gruff and Little billy goat Gruff.

Big billy goat Gruff was a very big goat. He had a thick, black coat and very large horns. He walked with his head high in the air. He was very proud and was not frightened of anything.

Middle billy goat Gruff was smaller than Big billy goat Gruff. He had a shiny, brown coat and small horns. His coat was very shiny and it glistened in the sunshine. He was always very busy looking after Little billy goat Gruff.

Little billy goat Gruff was very small. He was 8 months old. He had a very soft, white coat. He was very adventurous and he liked to explore new places. He often got lost.

The three billy goats Gruff lived in a beautiful country. There were high mountains. Big billy goat liked to climb.

There were also plenty of fields. The fields had lush, green grass. Middle billy goat like to eat lush, green grass.

This country had lots of pine trees. Birds nested in the pine trees. Little billy goat like to chase the birds.

The winters were very cold. It often snowed, and the goats sheltered in a cave to keep warm. The summers were warm and sunny. The birds sang every day in the summer.

The three billy goats Gruff liked spring best. In the spring the snow melted, and the streams were full of water. In the spring the grass grew again and was very sweet. In the spring the flowers and herbs began to grow and fill the air with scent.

It was the first day of spring. The three billy goats Gruff left their cave. They went to look for some sweet, green grass. They walked all morning. The birds sang in the trees. The goats smelt the first flowers and tasted the first herbs.

Eventually they came to a river. The snow was melting. The river was full of cool, clear water. On the other side of the river was a meadow. The meadow was full of lush, green grass. The grass was just perfect. The goats' tummies began to rumble.

Nearby was an old, wooden bridge over the river. Under this bridge lived a fierce and ugly troll. He listened for footsteps on the bridge. On the wooden bridge footsteps made the sound trip, trap, trip, trap. The troll jumped out and gobbled up whoever was crossing the bridge.

The three billy goats Gruff were very frightened of the troll. Even Big Billy Goat Gruff was afraid.

Part 2

A little later Little billy goat Gruff started to fidget. He ran across the field and back again. He jumped in the air. He was bored. He looked at the bridge.

"I don't want to stay on this side," said Little billy goat Gruff to himself, "I want to cross the bridge to the other side."

Little billy goat Gruff decided to cross the bridge by himself.

Trip, trap, trip, trap, Little billy goat Gruff's hooves tapped on the wooden bridge. He bravely trotted half way across the bridge.

Suddenly the ugly troll jumped up on to the bridge. He stood in front of Little billy goat Gruff.

"Who is trip-trapping over my bridge?" roared the troll.

"It's only me," whimpered the little goat, "I am Little billy goat Gruff. I need to cross the bridge because I want to eat the lush, green grass in the meadow."

"Oh no, you're not!" bellowed the fierce troll, "because I am going to gobble you all up!" The troll grabbed at Little billy goat Gruff.

"Stop, stop!" the little goat shouted with his biggest voice. "Please don't eat me, I am only small. Wait for a bigger goat!"

Little billy goat quickly ran past the troll and skipped in to the meadow with the sweet, green grass.

Middle billy goat Gruff looked up and saw Little billy goat on the other side. He was very worried and went to the bridge at once.

"I must cross the bridge to be with Little billy goat," he said to himself.

Trip, trap, trip, trap, trip trap, Middle billy goat Gruff's hooves tapped on the wooden bridge. He cautiously trotted half way across the bridge.

Suddenly the ugly troll jumped up on to the bridge. He stood in front of Middle billy goat Gruff.

"Who is trip-trapping over my bridge?" the troll roared with his angry voice.

"It's only me," said the goat softly, "I am Middle billy goat Gruff. I need to cross the bridge to be with Little billy goat in the lush, green meadow."

"Oh no, you're not!" yelled the ugly troll, "because I am going to gobble you all up!" The troll lunged at Middle billy goat Gruff.

"SSSStop, sssstop!" the frightened goat stammered. "PPPPlease don't eat me, I am not very fat. WWWWait for a bigger goat!"

Middle billy goat quickly ran past the troll and skipped in to the meadow with the sweet, green grass. He went straight to Little billy goat Gruff and together they ate the sweet grass.

Big billy goat looked up and saw Middle billy goat and Little billy goat on the other side.

"If they can cross the bridge, so can I!" laughed Big billy goat to himself.

Trip, trap, trip, trap, trip, trap, trip, trap, Big billy goat Gruff's hooves tapped on the wooden bridge. He confidently trotted half way across the bridge.

Suddenly the ugly troll jumped up on to the bridge. He stood in front of Big billy goat Gruff.

"Who is trip-trapping over my bridge?" the troll bellowed with a deep voice.

"It's me," challenged the goat, "I am Big billy goat Gruff. I want to cross the bridge to eat the lush, green grass in the meadow."

"Oh no, you're not!" answered the hungry troll, "because I am going to gobble you all up!"

"Oh no, you're not!" growled Big billy goat Gruff, "because I am going to gobble you all up!"

Big billy goat lowered his head. His horns pointed towards the troll. Then he charged towards the ugly troll. Bang, bang, bang, clattered the huge goat's hooves on the wooden bridge.

The troll did not escape. Big billy goat Gruff butted him. He tossed the troll high in to the air with his horns.

SPLASH! The troll landed in the water below. The water was flowing fast. The troll was quickly carried far, far away.

Big billy goat gruff raised his head and proudly crossed the bridge.

Middle billy goat and Little billy goat ran to him, they were very happy. The troll had not eaten Big billy goat Gruff. Big billy goat Gruff had thrown the troll off the bridge.

The ugly troll was never seen again. Anyone could cross the bridge safely now.

The three billy goats Gruff ate lots of the sweet, green grass and became very fat goats indeed!

The End

Comprehension Questions

Answer the following questions about the story.

1. What colour was Big billy goat Gruff's coat?
2. What colour was Middle billy goat Gruff's coat?
3. How old was Little billy goat Gruff?
4. What colour was Little billy goat's coat?
5. Which type of trees grew in their country?
6. Where did the goats shelter in the winter?
7. Who sang in the summers?
8. Which was the goats' favourite season?
9. What happened in the spring?
10. What was on the other side of the river?
11. What was the bridge across the river made from?
12. Who lived under the bridge?
13. What did the troll dohu to anyone on the bridge?
14. Who tried to cross the bridge first?
15. What sound did the goats' hooves make on the bridge?
16. What excuse did Little billy goat make to stop the troll eating him?

17. Which goat crossed the bridge next?
18. Why did he want to cross the bridge?
19. What excuse did Middle billy goat make to stop the troll eating him?
20. What sound did Big billy goat's hooves make when he charged at the troll?
21. What did he use to butt the troll with?
22. Where did the troll land?
23. What happened to the troll?
24. Who could cross the bridge now?
25. What did the goats do in the meadow?

Vocabulary Questions

1. Write a sentence using each of the following words:

A) horns

B) explore

C) grass

D) snow

E) wooden

2. Three seasons are described in the story. Write a sentence about each season:

3. **The story describes a beautiful country. List 5 words used to describe this beautiful country:**

4. **Look through the story and choose a verb from the list to complete the sentences below:**

- *stammered yelled laughed roared whimpered*

A) "Who is trip-trapping over my bridge?" __________ the troll.

B) "I am Little billy goat Gruff," __________ the little goat

C) "SSSStop, sssstop!" __________ the little goat.

D) "I am going to gobble you all up!" __________ the ugly troll.

E) "If they can cross the bridge, so can I!" __________ Big billy goat.

5. **Give 2 alternatives for the following words:**

A) thick

B) shiny

C) scent

D) eventually

E) fierce

Grammar Questions

1. Change the following sentences into the present continuous tense:

A) Little billy goat Gruff enjoyed new places.
B) The goats sheltered in a cave to keep warm.
C) The troll did not escape.
D) The birds sang in the trees.
E) Big billy goat Gruff tossed the troll in the air.

2. Underline the subject and circle the object in the following sentences:

A) Middle billy goat Gruff looked after Little billy goat Gruff.
B) Little billy goat explored new places.
C) The goats looked for some sweet, green grass.
D) They tasted the first herbs.
E) The troll grabbed at Little billy goat Gruff.

3. Change the following sentences from positive to negative:

A) Middle billy goat's coat glistened in the sunshine.
B) Little billy goat Gruff was very adventurous.
C) They walked all morning.
D) The goats' tummies rumbled.
E) The ugly troll jumped up on the bridge.

Writing Practice

1. Re-write the story in your own words.
2. Little billy goat Gruff was very adventurous. Write about an adventure from another day.
3. Write about what happened to the troll after he was tossed off the bridge.

Glossary

Part 1

once upon a time: a traditional beginning for stories.

billy goat: a male goat.

lush: sweet and juicy.

tummy rumbling: a sign of hunger.

troll: a fictional character from Scandinavian legends, usually a dwarf.

trip, trap: represents a tapping sound.

gobble up: to eat quickly.

Part 2

butted: to push hard with the head.

Level: 2

Goldilocks And 'he Three Bears

Part 1

Once upon a time three bears lived together in a house. The house was in the middle of a forest. There was Daddy Bear, Mummy Bear and Baby Bear. One morning the bears woke up. It was a lovely spring morning. They quickly got up and went downstairs.

"I am going to make some porridge for breakfast today," said Mummy Bear.

"I will help you," said Baby Bear.

Together Mummy Bear and Baby Bear made porridge for breakfast. Daddy bear lit the fire. Then he sat in his chair and read the newspaper.

"Daddy Bear, breakfast is ready!" called Baby Bear, "come to the table."

The three bears sat at the table to eat their porridge.

"My porridge is too hot," cried Baby Bear.

"My porridge is too hot," said Mummy Bear.

"My porridge is too hot," agreed Daddy Bear, "let's go for a walk. Then our porridge will be cool."

The three bears stood up. They left their house and went for a walk in the forest.

During this time a little girl came to their house. The little girl had long blonde hair and her name was Goldilocks. She was a very pretty girl but she was also very nosy.

"I wonder who lives here?" she said to herself. She walked along the path to the door. She knocked on the door, but there was no answer.

This did not stop Goldilocks. She was very nosy and wanted to look inside the house.

"I will open the door and peep inside," she told herself.

Goldilocks opened the door and looked inside. However she did not shut the door again because she wanted to see more. She went inside the house and called out. But no-one answered.

She wandered into the living room. There was a fire in the fireplace. It was lovely and warm in the bear's house. Goldilocks saw three chairs in the living room; a big, wooden chair, a medium-sized, flowery, old armchair, and a small bright-coloured chair.

"I walked a long way this morning. I will sit down and rest for a while," she told herself. Goldilocks sat in Daddy Bear's big chair.

"This chair is too hard," thought Goldilocks. She looked around and saw Mummy Bear's chair.

"I will try this chair," Goldilocks said and she sat in Mummy Bear's chair.

"This chair is too lumpy," she said and she stood up again. Then she saw Baby Bear's chair.

"I will try this chair," Goldilocks decided. She sat in Baby Bear's chair.

"This is perfect, very comfy. I will rest here for a little while."

But Goldilocks was too heavy for Baby Bear's chair. Suddenly the chair broke and Goldilocks fell on the floor.

"Oh dear," she cried and stood up, "I will do something else. I am hungry."

Goldilocks walked into the kitchen and saw the three bowls of porridge on the table.

"I like porridge," she said, "I will just eat a little."

Goldilocks went to Daddy Bear's bowl and tasted the porridge.

"Yuk!" she said, "this porridge is too salty!"

Goldilocks went to Mummy Bear's bowl and tasted the porridge.

"Yuk!" she said, "this porridge is too sweet!"

Goldilocks went to Baby Bear's bowl and tasted the porridge.

"Yummy!" she said, "this porridge is just right!"

Goldilocks liked Baby Bear's porridge very much and ate it all.

Goldilocks yawned.

"I am tired now," she said, "I will go upstairs and lie down for a little while."

Goldilocks climbed up the stairs in the three bears' house. She went into the bedroom and saw three beds; a big bed, a medium-sized bed and a small bed.

She lay down on Daddy Bear's big bed.

"Oh no, this bed is too hard and cold," moaned Goldilocks.

She got up and went to Mummy Bear's medium-sized bed.

"Oh no, this bed is too soft," complained Goldilocks.

She got up again and went to Baby Bear's small bed.

"This bed is perfect," she said, "it is soft and warm."

Goldilocks yawned again and quickly fell asleep.

Part 2

Meanwhile the three bears enjoyed their walk in the forest. The sun was warm and the sky was blue. The birds sang in the trees. It was the first day of spring.

Baby Bear ran among the trees and picked some flowers. He gave the flowers to Mummy Bear.

"Thank you Baby Bear," she said, and kissed him.

Daddy Bear liked to watch the birds.

"Listen!" whispered Daddy Bear, "I heard a woodpecker. Can you see it?"

"Over there, in that old oak tree," replied Mummy Bear.

"I can see it too," said Baby Bear.

The bears continued along the forest path.

"I am hungry now, can we go home?" pleaded Baby Bear.

"Yes, let's go home," decided Daddy Bear.

The three bears walked home again, singing their favourite song. They soon came back to their own little garden.

"Look," shouted Baby Bear, "the door is open. Someone has been here."

The three bears crept back into the house.

"Look!" whispered Daddy Bear, "someone sat in my chair."

"Look!" whispered Mummy Bear, "someone sat in my chair."

"Look!" cried Baby Bear, "someone sat in my chair, and they broke it!" Baby Bear started to cry.

"Don't worry," Mummy Bear comforted him, "Daddy Bear will mend it for you."

The three bears went into the kitchen.

"Look!" said Daddy Bear, "someone ate some of my porridge."

"Look!" said Mummy Bear, "someone ate some of my porridge."

"Look!" said Baby Bear, "someone ate my porridge, and they ate it all up!" Baby Bear started to cry again.

"Don't worry," comforted Mummy Bear, "I will make some more porridge for you."

The three bears climbed up the stairs and went into their bedroom.

"Look!" said Daddy Bear, "someone lay on my bed."

"Look!" said Mummy Bear, "someone lay on my bed."

"Look!" whispered Baby Bear, "someone lay on my bed, and she's still here, fast asleep!"

Goldilocks woke up suddenly, and saw the three bears. She jumped up, ran down the stairs and out of the house. She ran all the way home.

The End

Comprehension Questions

Answer the following questions about the story.

1. Where do the bears live?
2. Which season is it?
3. What do the bears do before going downstairs?
4. What does Mummy Bear say she will make for breakfast?
5. Why don't the bears eat their breakfast?
6. What does Daddy Bear suggest they do?
7. Who visits the house?
8. What colour is the visitor's hair?
9. Which room did Goldilocks enter first?
10. Why didn't she like Mummy Bear's chair?
11. What happened when she sat in Baby Bear's chair?
12. Which room did Goldilocks go to next?
13. Why didn't she like Daddy Bear's porridge?
14. Goldilocks ate Baby Bear's porridge. She was tired. How do we know?
15. Why did Goldilocks not like Daddy Bear's bed?
16. How do we know she liked Baby Bear's bed?
17. What did Baby Bear give to his Mum in the forest?

18. What did Daddy Bear enjoy doing in the forest?
19. Which type of bird did they see?
20. How did they know someone visited the house?
21. Baby Bear saw his broken chair. What did he do?
22. The bears went to the kitchen. What did Daddy Bear say?
23. Baby Bear's bowl was empty. What did Mummy Bear say to him?
24. The bears went upstairs. Whose bed was Goldilocks asleep in?
25. What did Goldilocks do when she woke up?

Vocabulary Questions

1. Write a sentence using each of the following words:

A) forest

B) spring

C) porridge

D) kitchen

E) stairs

2. **Daddy Bear heard a woodpecker in the forest. Name 5 other types of bird: (use a dictionary)**

3. **List 5 rooms in a typical house. For each room list 2 things normally found there: (use a dictionary)**

4. **Add the correct question word to these questions:**

   A) __________ aren't you eating your porridge?

   B) I wonder __________ lives here?

   C) __________ tree is the woodpecker in?

   D) __________ has happened to my chair?

   E) __________ is sleeping in my bed?

5. **Give 2 alternatives for the following words:**

   A) quickly

   B) shut

   C) to moan

   D) lovely

   E) big

Grammar Questions

1. Change the following sentences into the past tense:

A) Daddy Bear is waking up.

B) Mummy Bear is making porridge.

C) Baby Bear is running in the forest.

D) Mummy Bear is hungry.

E) Goldilocks is sleeping in Baby Bear's bed.

2. Underline the adjectives in the following sentences:

A) Daddy Bear has a big chair.

B) Mummy Bear does not have salty porridge.

C) Baby Bear sat in his soft, small chair.

D) Goldilocks did not like the lumpy chair.

E) Little Baby Bear ran happily along the forest path.

3. Change the following sentences from positive to negative:

A) Mummy Bear woke up first.

B) Daddy Bear suggested porridge for breakfast.

C) Goldilocks closed the door.

D) Baby Bear started to cry.

E) Goldilocks broke the chair.

Writing Practice

1. Re-write the story in your own words.
2. Goldilocks told her friend about her visit to the bear's house. Write about the conversation.
3. Goldilocks' mother told her to go back to the bear's house, and to say sorry. Write about what happened.

Glossary

Part 1

once upon a time: a traditional beginning for stories.

porridge: made with warm milk and oats.

nosy: curious or inquisitive.

peep: to look quickly.

for a while: for a period of time.

comfy: comfortable.

yuk: to dislike a food.

yummy: to like a food.

just right: perfect.

fell asleep: started to sleep.

PART 2

meanwhile: at the same time.

ate it all up: ate everything.

fast asleep: in a deep sleep.

Level: 3

The Three Little Pigs

Part 1

Once upon a time three little pigs lived with their mother. They all lived together in a big house. The first little pig was called Jack. He was a very clever little pig. He enjoyed maths and science.

The second little pig was called David. He was a happy little pig. He enjoyed stories about animals.

The third little pig was called Robin. He was a very lazy little pig. He liked to lie in the sunshine and eat.

One day the mother called her three little pigs. She said, "My darlings, you are growing up. It is time for you to leave me and to make your own homes."

The next day the three little pigs packed their bags. Jack put some tools and a map in his bag. David put some books and toys in his bag. Robin put some sandwiches and biscuits in his bag.

The three little pigs said goodbye to their mother. She felt very sad and prayed for them to be safe.

"Don't worry," said Jack "I will build a strong house."

"Don't worry," said David "I will be happy with my books."

"Don't worry," said Robin "I will not be hungry."

The three little pigs set off along the road. They walked all day. In the evening they made a fire. They sat together and soon fell asleep.

In the morning David looked at his map.

"I can see a nice big field. I will build my house there. But it will take two hours to walk there from here."

Robin was tired, and he did not want to walk any further.

"I like it here," he said "I am going to build my house here."

Jack and David said goodbye to Robin and set off on their way. Robin thought about his house.

"How will I build my house?" he wondered. He looked and looked. At last he found some straw in a field.

"I will build a nice house with this straw," he decided. "I will finish it quickly and then I will sit in the sunshine."

Robin started work. He quickly built a simple house. Afterwards he opened his bag. He took out his sandwiches and biscuits, and ate them. Then he fell asleep in the sunshine.

Jack and David walked along the road. It was a hot day and David was tired. They saw a river.

"I want to have a drink," said David. The two little pigs sat down on the grass beside the river.

"Come on, let's go!" said Jack.

"I am too tired," said David, "I am going to build my house here beside the river."

Jack said goodbye to David and set off on his way. David thought about his house.

"What can I use to build my house?" he wondered. He looked and looked. At last he found some sticks in a forest.

"I will build a nice house with these sticks", he decided, "I will finish it quickly, and then I will read a book."

David started work. He built a nice house. His house had a window and a door. Afterwards he opened his bag. He took out his books and toys. He played with his toys and then read a book.

Jack walked and walked. At last he saw a big, flat field.

"I will build my house here," he decided.

"How will I build my house?" he wondered. He looked and looked. At last he found some bricks in the corner of the field.

"I will build a good, strong house with these bricks," he decided, "I will work hard."

Jack started work. He worked for 2 days. He built a good, strong house with windows, a door and a chimney.

In the evening he was very tired. He cooked a meal over a fire in the fireplace. He ate the meal, locked the door and then he went to bed.

Part 2

Not far away lived a wolf. The wolf lived in a cave and everyday he hunted for food.

On this morning the wolf woke up. He was very hungry.

"I am going to find a nice little pig to eat," he decided.

The wolf left his cave and walked across the fields. Soon he came to Robin's house. Robin was outside the house, lying in the sunshine.

Robin heard a noise and looked up. He did not see anyone. He was afraid and ran inside his house.

The wolf laughed, "you silly little pig, do you think you are safe from me in your house?"

The wolf walked to Robin's house. "This house is made of straw!" the wolf scoffed, "I will easily blow it down!"

"I will huff and puff and blow your house down," the wolf shouted to the little pig.

The wolf huffed and puffed and blew down the straw house.

But Robin was very quick and he ran out from the back of the house. He ran and ran. At last he arrived at David's house.

"David, David!" called Robin.

"What has happened?" asked David.

"A big, bad wolf came and blew my house down."

"Don't worry, stay with me," said David.

The wolf went back to his cave. He was very angry. He did not have any supper.

The next day the wolf woke up. He was very, very hungry.

"Today I am going to find a nice little pig to eat," he decided.

The wolf left his cave and walked and walked. At

last the wolf came to David's house. David and Robin hid inside the house. They saw the wolf.

The wolf was very happy.

"There are two pigs in this house and I am very, very hungry," he thought.

"This house is made of sticks!" the wolf scoffed, "I will easily blow it down!"

"I will huff and puff and blow your house down," the wolf shouted to the two little pigs.

The wolf huffed and puffed and blew down the stick house.

But Robin and David were very quick and they ran out from the back of the house. They ran and ran. At last they arrived at Jack's house.

They knocked on the door.

"Please let us in!" they shouted

Jack opened the door and Robin and David ran inside.

"A wolf came and blew my house down," said Robin.

"A wolf came and blew my house down," said David.

"Don't worry, my house is strong. You will stay here with me," Jack told them.

The wolf went back to his cave. He was very, very angry. He did not have any supper again.

The next day the wolf woke up. He was very, very, very hungry.

"Today I am going to find a nice little pig to eat," he decided.

The wolf left his cave and walked and walked and walked. Eventually the wolf came to Jack's house. Jack, David and Robin hid inside the house. They saw the wolf.

Jack's house was strong and the three little pigs were not afraid.

"I will huff and puff and blow your house down," the wolf shouted to the three little pigs.

The wolf huffed and puffed, but nothing happen. Then the wolf had an idea. He climbed on the roof and into the chimney.

Inside the house there was a big pan of boiling water over the fire.

The wolf fell down the chimney and into the pan. The water was very hot. The wolf howled with pain. He jumped out of the pan, ran out of the front door, and ran and ran.

"That wolf will not come back again!" cheered Jack.

The three little pigs lived happily ever after in Jack's strong, brick house.

The End

Comprehension Questions

Answer the following questions about the story.

1. In the beginning who did the three little pigs live with?
2. Describe Jack.
3. Describe David.
4. Describe Robin.
5. What did Jack put in his bag?
6. What did David put in his bag?
7. What did Robin put in his bag?
8. Was their mother upset when her three little pigs left?
9. Where did they stop at the end of the first day?
10. What did Robin use to build his house?
11. Where did Jack and David stop to have a drink?
12. What did David make his house with?
13. David finished his house. What did he do next?
14. Where did Jack build his house?
15. What did Jack make his house with?
16. Jack finished his house. What did he do next?

17. Where did the wolf live?
18. What happened when the wolf found the first little pig?
19. How did Robin escape?
20. The following day whose house did the wolf find?
21. Who was inside the house?
22. What did the wolf do to the house?
23. How did Robin and David escape?
24. The next day whose house did the wolf find?
25. What happened when the wolf climbed down the chimney?

Vocabulary Questions

1. Write a sentence using each of the following words:

A) clever

B) map

C) lazy

D) cave

E) build

2. Pigs are usually farm animals. Name 5 other types of farm animal: (use a dictionary)

3. The pigs walked near a river. List 5 other places where water is found: (use a dictionary)

4. Change the underlined word(s) for the correct pronoun:

A) Jack enjoyed maths and science.

B) The three little pigs lived with their mother.

C) Their mother was sad on the day the pigs left.

D)'Jack and I will carry on walking,' said David.

E) The wolf lived in a cave.

5. Give 2 alternatives for the following words:

A) clever

B) sad

C) simple

D) sound

E) angry

Grammar Questions

1. Change the following sentences into the future tense:

A) The three little pigs lived in a big house.
B) Jack built a strong house.
C) Robin was hungry.
D) The wolf blew the house down.
E) The three pigs lived happily ever after.

2. Underline the verb*(s)* in the following sentences:

A) "My darlings, you are growing up," said their mother.
B) Jack put some tools and a map in his bag.
C) In the evening they made a fire.
D) The wolf did not have any supper.
E) The wolf climbed on the roof.

3. Change the following sentences from positive to negative:

A) Robin liked to read stories about animals.

B) Their mother was happy.

C) Jack built his house with straw.

D) The wolf was friendly.

E) The wolf ate the pigs.

Writing Practice

1. Re-write the story in your own words.
2. Jack kept a diary. Write his account of the events.
3. The wolf ran away from Jack's house. Write about what happened to him afterwards.

Glossary

PART 1

once upon a time: a traditional beginning for stories that are not in a real setting.

fall asleep: to start to sleep.

PART2

scoff : to laugh at.

huff and puff: to take a big breath and blow.

at last: the same as 'eventually', or 'in a while'

lived happily ever after: a traditional ending for stories like this one. It means that they were always happy.

account: report.